Our F

Contents

MW01518362

Our Senses

We have five senses.
Our senses tell us about
things around us.

Our Five Senses

sight

hearing

smell

touch

taste

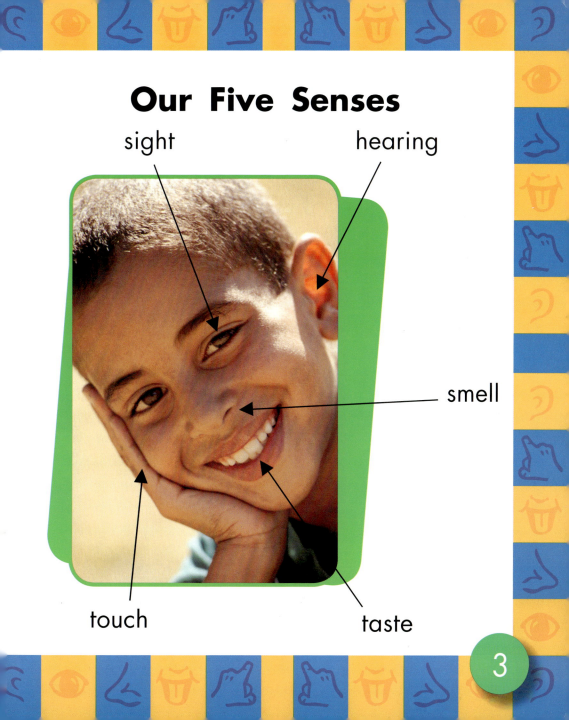

Sight

We use our eyes to see.
Our sense of sight tells
us how things look.

Our eyes
see colors.

Our eyes
see shapes
and sizes.

Our eyes see
light and dark.

5

Smell

We use our nose to smell things around us.

How do these things smell?

Hearing

Our ears hear.
Our sense of hearing
tells us about the sounds
around us.

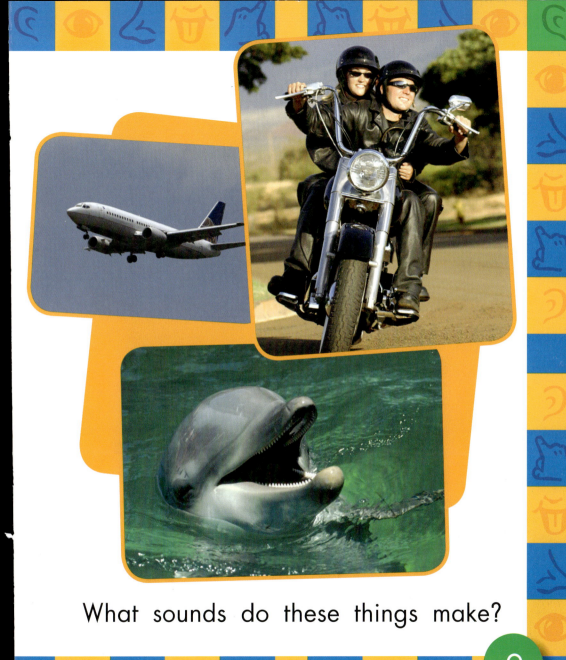

What sounds do these things make?

Taste

We use our tongues to taste. Our sense of taste tells us when food is sweet, sour, bitter, or salty.

How do these foods taste?

Each part of our tongue tells us how foods taste.

sour   salty   sweet   bitter

Touch

We touch with our skin. Our sense of touch tells us how things feel.

What ways do we
use our sense of touch?

13

Senses in Action

We use our senses every day.

Which of our senses are used
in each picture?

Index